I'll Buy Flowers Again Tomorrow

Charlotte Lit Press
Charlotte Center for Literary Arts, Inc.
PO Box 18607
Charlotte, NC 28218
charlottelit.org/press

Cover photo by Patricia Ann Joslin
Author photo by Kathryn G. Pickard

ISBN: 978-1-960558-01-5

PROUD MEMBER

COMMUNITY OF LITERARY MAGAZINES & PRESSES
W W W . C L M P . O R G

I'll Buy Flowers Again Tomorrow

Poems of Loss and Healing

Patricia Ann Joslin

CHARLOTTELIT

P   R   E   S   S

Charlotte Center for Literary Arts, Inc.
Charlotte, North Carolina
charlottelit.org

In loving memory of Roy H. Joslin
1951 - 2018

husband
father
grandfather

Be patient where you sit in the dark. The dawn is coming.
                                                        ~Rumi

Contents

Loss

November, One Year After

Table set for one. A single glass, one plate, one year. Knife
and fork stand guard in this castle-apartment I call home.
I drain the dregs of zinfandel opened two days ago. Old
vine now bitter. *Should I open another bottle?* Turned the
clock back yesterday, seconds slipped away. Day winds
down into darkness. The wind whispers your name.

**

We would not have crafted this meal together. You didn't
care for fish, craved spice and salt though your body
rebelled. Perhaps you might have sampled crusty bread
like the just-out-of-the-oven baguette we bought at that
boulangerie in Sarlat. We devoured it, then returned for
another. I think of you, broken, beautiful.

**

Red-and-yellow-tinged roses in this crystal vase crumple
like last week's newspapers. I picture our house on the
river, its once lush garden now overgrown by chickweed
and clover. Even so, daffodils bloom after winter darkness.
Traces of oil paint portraits across the surface of this empty
plate, my glass half full. I'll buy flowers again tomorrow.

Kintsugi

I trudge through campus
alone, shattered by loss.
Like a Japanese craftsman
you soften my edges,
pour gold to seal my cracks,
polish, cradle me.
You mend me
to become beautiful,
dust me with desire,
create a shining cup
for us to share,
fragments fixed by fate.
I surrender
to your artistry.

Remembrance: Roy Joslin

I didn't think to write an obituary.

The notice about the memorial
service and burial simply read:

> *Born. Died.*
> *Survived by wife.*
> *Columbarium.*

Family and friends
traveled far to honor him,
our son delivered a eulogy,
our daughter and I wept.

Now years have tarnished
the nameplate on his niche,
weathered the bench
in the church garden.

It's time to tell his story.

Words Are Not Enough

after "The Promise" by Tracy Chapman

Mike delivered a eulogy, crafted with his sister
between hymns and scripture
after words by the minister
before the Tracy Chapman song
you chose to tell us your promise.

He spoke of you as an engaged parent,
a man of great depth and spirit,
said your love for family
was unconditional, your eclectic taste
in music extended from blues to feminist rock.

He recounted your Dad jokes,
your delight in light-up Santas,
the time you lost your hair after chemo
then donned a costume beard
for a photo to post on CaringBridge.

Roy, words are not enough—
we miss your touch, your warm embrace,
the smell of your risotto on the stove,
the sound of champagne bottles
popping to ring in the New Year.

**

Jen remembers basketball games
on our sloping driveway, picking apples
each fall, the way you looked at her
the night the two of you danced
at her wedding.

Mike remembers your father-son
ski trips to Colorado, regular jaunts
to the ER for stitches,
working together
to hang the Christmas lights.

They snuggled with you
while watching X-Files and MacGyver,
learned to ride bikes on the trail,
skated at Gro Tonka park,
enjoyed vacations you planned
to snorkel, zip line, and boulder climb.

They think of counting stars
as a young family camping at Big Bay,
summer excursions to Cove Point Lodge,
the Costa Rica trip as adults
when we partied late into the night
on New Year's Eve.

They recall your wise advice
to grow from *character-building experiences*—
like the time Jen was escorted home
by a policewoman, and the time
Mike ended up in a ditch
after drinking and maybe saw an angel.

Roy, you fill a space in our hearts,
so many tales to tell our grandchildren—
a mélange of memories to remind us
of the incredible man you were.

Sunrise Over Fisher Peak

Last night heat lightning—
fire-breath explosions from chimera clouds
ricocheted across distant ridges.

Today dawn dark, stars fade—
then, faint horizon over the hills,
a slow dance to imagined music.

In silence we sip coffee,
watch new day ignite then catapult
like wildfire over Fisher Peak.

Unafraid to Hope

Now faith is the assurance of things hoped for,
the conviction of things not seen.
Hebrews 11:1

He was—
hero to the end
unafraid to learn
the truth of it
unafraid to face Death
yet fearful of the mess
of dying, departing.
       God, I am strong!

I was—
champion to the end
unafraid to hear
his weeping song
to soothe him—
hold him, caress
bathe him, dress
feed him
sweet portions, potions.
       God, I am strong!

We were—
courageous to the end
unafraid to hope
until his ravaged body
wasted away in a last gasp
as I held him fast,
as I cried out
       God, take him now!

Carved

I wear his ring tonight—
one of two, mine stolen
by the thief who pillaged
our home.

Ancient text etched in gold,
love carved into contour,
burnished by sweet kisses,
scrubbed by daily living.

I wear his ring tonight
on this anniversary eve,
my hands are cold
and knuckled.

Wounded

How fast the body healed
the deep gouge on my right thumb
from the box grater, bandaged
two days, scabbed on the third

and the spider bite that scarred
my left ankle, souvenir
of our stroll through the trees
when we were young, carefree.

Last night I dreamt
you gripped a chainsaw
lopped tree limbs
until you collapsed
under their weight
crushed

dead again.

The Vocabulary of Cancer

back pain
appointments
diagnosis
pancreas
oncologist
5-FU
Caringbridge
platelets
neuropathy
Creon
Atropin
nutritionist
blood pressure
Senna
PT
potassium
infection
lesions
fever
Xarelto
endoscopy
pastoral visits

family first
surgery
port
chemo
anxiety
cancer marker
friends
Mirtazapin
foot tremors
floating stools
Fenergan
Boost Plus
pressure points
Dronabinol
paracentesis
muscle tone
Amoxicillin
liver
tears
Reglan
blood clots
prayer

fatigue
denial
Stage IV
options
headache
CA 19-9
massage
magnesium
hair loss
hiccups
Zofran
milkshakes
insurance
Compazine
ER
atrophy
pneumonia
mineral oil
social worker
Gemzar
Pantoprazole
planning

Why?
decisions
What if?
palliative care
Irinotecan
nausea
lymphedema
Baclofen
CT scans
Decadron
How?
Lactulose
restless legs
compression socks
spirometer
x rays
Xeloda
statistics
Abraxane
When?
family
last

pain
hemoglobin
enema
Docusate
Leucovorin
nightmares
Lasix
bed pillow
cane
acupuncture
home care
Lorazepam
walker
shower chair
ultrasound
depression
wheelchair
Neulasta
Haldol
withering
morphine
breath

weight loss
tumors
anemia
Oxaliplatin
malaise
neutrophils
dehydration
bills
tinea
thrush
Medicare
Zenpep
Biofreeze
wheeze
cirrhosis
Lexapro
lethargy
hospice
DNR
weakness
sleep
death

Mother, I Sing of You

You held me close within your heart
that Sunday morning of my birth,
blessed by God, you were set apart

as Mother, teenage matriarch.
Through infant play then childish ways
you held me close within your heart.

I pulled away—a selfish start
from mother, brothers, father, kin.
Blessed by God, I was set apart

to climb alone, my life to chart.
Then first love died, just twenty-five,
you held me close within your heart.

You held me close til healing's start,
when new love bloomed, then motherhood.
Blessed by God, you were set apart

until life ebbed, a time to part,
you orphaned me yet left your love.
You held me close within your heart,
blessed by God, we were set apart.

Healing

Springtime in the Columbarium

daffodils droop beside
this bench emblazoned with
your nameplate, end date

chill creeps under my collar
wet shadows linger
cardinals squall beyond the wall

I recall the bold redbird
that pecked at our window
for weeks after you died

knocked and knocked
until I sold the house
and moved away

**

pink Yoshino blooms
stipple these stone walls

hydrangeas unfurl leaves
over dusty loam

Koreanspice viburnum
dispatches its sweetness

azalea buds pucker
wait to burst into bloom

Welcoming William

We gathered on a warm April night
in a darkened delivery room—
two grandmothers and a doula.

Beloved, you died months ago
before this child was even a whisper

but it was you who rallied us that night
as our son-in-law donned the tattered
orange shirt you wore to fire up
your Clemson Tigers—

a beacon to encourage Jennifer
with your presence, a gift
to lift us all as labor lasted,
her pain-tired patience grew thin.

You emboldened our girl
        to the final push that propelled
                my heart to ricochet

shaken with grief
shattered by bliss.

September in the Garden

On Saturday I took friends
to see the gardens at our old house,
a place on the river just out from town
where summertime gardenia, daisies,
daylilies multiplied by magic
and fall lantana grew tall.

In my city apartment
I now tend pots
of rosemary, basil
sedum and chives.

We arrived, but
where once September
chrysanthemums grew,
we found only
crabgrass, spurge.

I was hobbled
by memories of that fall,
of your decline,
your dying, and after

when I walked
out of those gardens
without you.

I Didn't Mean to Write a Poem

I didn't mean to write a poem
but I did, instead of taking a walk
in the rain or doing laundry.

Mondays are my catch-up day—
bills, groceries, maybe baking
bread or making calls.

I only meant to change the battery
on the kitchen clock
that stopped last week

but as I turned back time I thought
of you in leisure suit and beard,
me with perm and bell-bottoms.

In a week you'll be dead
three years. I sleep alone
in the middle of our king bed

dreaming scenes of sunshine days,
flashes across time. Yet, family
portraits without you remind me

that you never knew grandsons two,
three, four, or broke par, traveled
to New Zealand as we planned.

I changed the clock battery—
time now ticks past the hour
of your passing, moving forward.

The Aerialist

Hope is the thing with feathers…
— *Emily Dickinson*

Weeks after your death a scarlet-cloaked
bird came tap-tapping on my window
        my pain red-raw

you arrived every morning for months—
you, raucous spirit-soul tied to the heavens
        my feet planted in tear-damp earth

your peck-peck-peck
branded me wife-widow
        no longer lover, partner, friend.

Today, three years on, you return as hummingbird
hovering beyond wrought iron balcony bars
        my ruby-throated visitor

midair acrobat, precision flier—
you court me in face-to-face
        shifts of your minute beating wings

        I stare back
        waiting
        to be caught.

Today at low tide

sea stars litter the shore, many stranded
in decay, others inch back
toward the safety of water's edge

terns and plovers scud the shoreline
ghost crabs scuttle the sand
waves pulsate a message, light massages me

the smell of death lingers
yet I savor the grainy bits between my toes—
like Eiseley's man on the Costabel beach

I become a star thrower

Sunday Morning on Seabrook Island

Alone on this gray May morning
I trek to the north point,
spot bottle-nose dolphins feeding
on mullets that flounder in shallows.
Sandpipers sweep this ancient shore.
Orange flags on the dunes mark
loggerhead nests, tracks to the sea
map the mothers' migration.
I curl the shoreline
in search of shells and memories.
Sandbar posts reveal themselves
as pelicans when I edge to the ocean,
leave footprints in wet sand,
mark my passing.

Senescence

my body, foot to top
is a masterpiece of engineering
though a work of fading art—
calendar pages abruptly recycle

my hair thins, sight crystalizes
like ice on the edge of a pond
veined calves cramp, toes encased
in thick bed socks freeze

my frame shrinks, face sags
my smile shines though teeth do not
my ears hear more or less
wanting only quiet, peace

my strong legs support tailbone,
torso, spine but no longer jog—
yet I still dance, hike the woods
crunch abs and glutes

when sleep enfolds me
I tango in Argentina
climb Kilimanjaro
dive off Kahekili's Leap

Lake Louise: Reflections at the Teahouse

In dreams lonely fog chills,
covers me, swallows me.
Entwined in white, I wake
embalmed.   Then, I doubt *You.*

Today I ford creek beds
ramble rock strewn trails
brush sweat from my eyes
breathe in lodgepole pines.

You, here as I wander
these winding woods, ascend
sun-dazed summit, breathless—
alone yet not alone.

Below, blue-green prism
reflects verdant forest
expansive azure skies.
On this blazing morning

You crown fields of fireweed
silence gray shadows
impassion with wonder.
Your creation conquers doubt.

Hiking the Blue Star

Along these root-ramped trails I search
for mock oysters, ringless
honey mushrooms, listen for songs
of wren, tufted titmouse

the click-click of acorns
underscore the dance of dry leaves
that cascade to blanket this crisp morning.

Here a fence lizard no longer than an eyebrow
there, yellow swallowtails swimming over
pink smartweed, joe-pye weed, boneset—
a nameless bird calling for its mate

its coo-hee not answered.
I summon you, beloved
buried too soon.

I shift the burden of the pack as it bites
into my shoulder, recall our September hikes—
the perfume of decay, shuffle-crunch of leaves
snap-pop of twigs, your warm hand in mine

and remember you in that photo—
your pale green jacket, gray bucket hat, head lifted
as you walk away from me into deep woods.

Understory Runes

As you ramble the path, regard the junctures,
choose a way to turn, then maybe turn back—
you will come to know the structure of the woods.

Notice the unfurled ferns, green-green moss,
wild mushrooms emerge from damp earth
alongside crushed leaves, pine needles.

Your feet may slough through mud and sludge—
beneath is not death but a place for newness.
Count the rings of age on the fallen oak.

Acknowledgements

Many thanks to the editors of the following publications in which versions of some of these poems first appeared:

Kakalak: "I Didn't Mean to Write a Poem" (2021) and "Hiking the Blue Star" (2022)

North Carolina Poetry Society's Poetry in Plain Sight: "Today at low tide"

Tipton Poetry Journal: "Kintsugi"

Sacred and Surprising: "Welcoming William"

Thanks to the editorial team at Charlotte Lit Press for their excellent work in bringing this chapbook to life.

I am deeply grateful for the Chapbook Lab experience at Charlotte Center for Literary Arts. In particular, I wish to thank teacher Dannye Romine Powell for her supportive and nurturing guidance throughout the lab experience, and to my mentor, Lola Haskins, for her expertise in shaping these poems with me. Our cohort group (Linda, Lucinda, Eric, Joe, Gary, Betty, Vivian, John, Brooke, and Kathie) have been therapists and friends throughout this endeavor. I am honored to count these fine poets as my inspiration as well as my cheerleaders.

The accomplished poets in my First Thursday writing group have helped me improve my craft and fine-tune many of the poems in this chapbook. In gratitude, I wish to acknowledge Brooke Lehmann, Cindy Buchanan, Bill Hollands, Seth Rosenbloom, Paula Stenberg, Judy Aks, and Kimberly Kralowec. Their own poems are widely published.

To my children, Jennifer and Michael, I give my heart and my soul. Their father would be so proud of them for the way they care for me!

About the Author

Patricia Ann Joslin grew up in the Midwest and now lives in Charlotte, North Carolina. Her poetry writing has been a venture of healing and personal growth. When not in Charlotte you may find her with grandsons in Maryland and Minnesota or on a tour in some faraway place, typically as a solo traveler. She loves the serenity of woodland hikes and the challenge of playing 18 holes of golf.

CPSIA information can be obtained
at www.ICGtesting.com
Printed in the USA
LVHW050723030523
745903LV00001B/2